# Baby and Beyond

## Progression in Play for Babies and Children

## Dolls and Soft Toys

# Baby and Beyond - Dolls and Soft Toys

ISBN 1-905019-80-7    •    978-1-905019-80-9

First published in the UK, January 2007

**'Baby and Beyond' is a trade mark of Featherstone Education Ltd**

Published in the United Kingdom by
Featherstone Education Ltd, 44 - 46 High Street, Husbands Bosworth, Leicestershire, LE17 6LP

*Printed in the UK on paper produced in the European Union from managed, sustainable forests*

# Contents

# Baby and Beyond

## A series of books for practitioners working with children from birth to five and beyond

This book gives ideas for introducing and extending role play activities and experiences for babies and young children. Each page spread contains a range of experiences and a selection of ideas for each of the developmental stages of the Early Years Foundation Stage (EYFS). We have retained the descriptive names of the four earlier developmental stages from Birth to Three Matters, while adjusting the age ranges to cover the whole EYFS:

| Birth - 11 months | 8 - 20 months | 16 - 26 months | 22 - 36 months | 30 - 60+ months |
|---|---|---|---|---|
| Heads up Lookers and Communicators | Sitters, Standers and Explorers | Movers, Shakers and Players | Walkers, Talkers and Pretenders | |

Dolls, soft toys (and puppets) are part of every child's life, wherever they live. In countries and places where children are less fortunate, they will make these friends from simple materials that they find. The baby blanket doll, the first teddy and the soft toy animal are features of children's lives from the moment they are born. Many babies form strong bonds with single toys, others gather a whole menagerie around them as they play and sleep. Still others seem to form no early attachment to dolls and soft toys, and wait for some time before suddenly fixing on one favourite. Dolls and soft toys share all the worries, stresses and important happenings of young children's lives, and are vital to the wellbeing and stability of many. However, dolls, soft toys and puppets are also key learning resources for practitioners to use to extend children's learning.

In this book, in addition to teddies, dolls and soft toy animals, we have included puppets and story characters that you can use in many different ways, right from the first days a baby spends in your setting. These early ideas include many that parents could also use. Any puppet or soft toy can become a character in their own story or a represent one in a well-loved picture book

The book also includes superheroes and modern dolls such as Barbie, because these have become firm favourites with children as they watch their stories on TV and in the cinema. These toys are a fact of modern life, and we should be using their strong appeal to support learning of all sorts, including the discussion of behaviour, social relationships, gender stereotypes and violent behaviour, encouraging children to see the difference between mindless violence and heroism.

Persona dolls are another type of doll to encourage thinking and empathy. They can be used right from the baby room, helping children to relate and engage with others outside themselves, with celebrations to share, problems and difficulties to solve.

We have also included sections on the important links between dolls and soft toys and other areas of activity. Using the dolls etc in role play, outdoor play, social development and empathy with others are all important roles these resources can play. Children can also develop the skills of thinking, designing, making, creating as they make accessories and homes for their friends. Fine motor skills can develop while pouring tea or doing up tiny fastenings; social and emotional development is supported when babies and children dress, bath, feed and look after dolls and other soft toy friends.

Of course, buying all the dolls, puppets and soft toys can be expensive, so we have included some ideas for making your own dolls and puppets with the children. These use cheap, familiar and readily available materials. The resulting characters will be loved and played with whatever their appearance. We know that we haven't included every idea, and haven't named all the suppliers. We mention a few key resources here - others can be obtained from bookshops or an internet search.

Resources and books:
The Little Book of Persona Dolls, The Little Book of Puppet Making, Beat Baby; *Featherstone Education* Tel: 01858 881213; *www.featherstone.uk.com*
Musical Toys for babies and children; *www.lamaze-uk.com*          Finger, glove, story and character puppets; *www.puppetsbypost.com*

| 0-11 months | 8-20 months | 16 - 26 months | 22 - 36 months | 30 - 60+ months |
| --- | --- | --- | --- | --- |

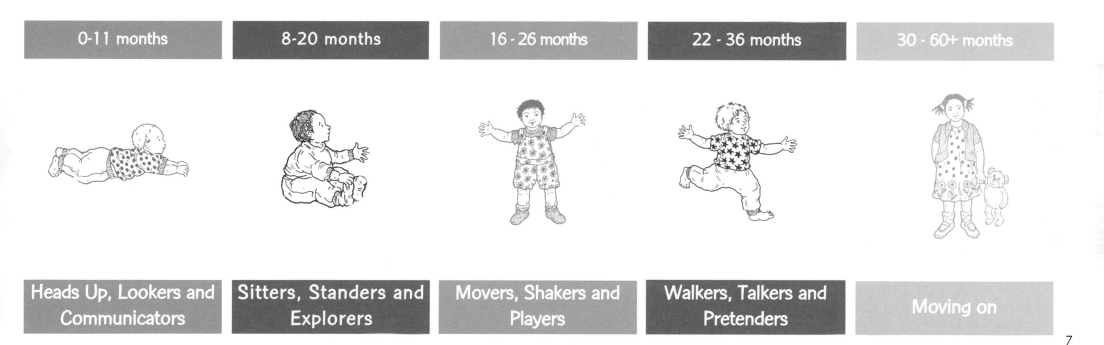

| Heads Up, Lookers and Communicators | Sitters, Standers and Explorers | Movers, Shakers and Players | Walkers, Talkers and Pretenders | Moving on |
| --- | --- | --- | --- | --- |

## Teddy

The first and lasting favourite for many children. These are the soft toys that adults keep, and are among the most popular bedtime and comfort toys. Teddies feature in hundreds of children's stories in many languages - they get lost, forgotten, sold by mistake. They are present at times of stress and loneliness, and share endless worries and secrets.

## Young babies (0-11 months)

Many young babies will already have a favourite teddy, and you may be able to welcome these comfort toys into your setting. If you can't include them in the daily routine, sit them on a high shelf where they can see what is going on and can be seen by their owners. Taking them down at changing time or rest time will be a good time for a short reunion during the day. If you can't have comfort toys from home, provide some soft, washable teddies.

### Heads Up, Lookers and Communicators

## Babies (8-20 months)

At this stage, babies will tend to pull toys along as they crawl or creep. Teddies need to be hard wearing and washable, with plenty of bits to hang on to. Arms, legs and ears will need to be firmly attached. They will also get sucked, so they must be washable! Involve the bears in suitable stories - there are so many stories about bears that you can share, making sure every child listening has a bear to cuddle as they listen to the story or song.

### Sitters, Standers and Explorers

## Young children (16-26 months)

Young children will still need bears around to join in the games children play as they begin to be more mobile. A simple Teddy Bears Picnic can be a focus for bear play, and stories about bears will continue to be popular. Encourage the children to carry bears in backpacks, baskets, baby walkers and barrows, and take them outside to sit on the grass or ride on the outside toys. These activities encourage care for others, while allowing for occasional enthusiastic handling or neglect!

**Movers, Shakers and Players**

## Children (22-36 months)

Introduce bears of various sizes and shapes as mathematical examples, counting, comparing and sorting different sorts. Use some familiar counting rhymes such as Five Brown Buns or Five Little Men in a Flying Saucer, and substitute bears for the usual objects, using real bears for the counting. Making name badges and talking about what different bears like to eat and do will prepare children for making up their own stories and songs.

**Walkers, Talkers and Pretenders**

## Older children (30-60+ months)

Try recording some teddy stories for the children to listen to independently, and leave a basket of bears in the quiet corner for children to choose from as they listen. Encourage children to make up stories about their own teddies and tell them to others. Photos of bears can be used for sorting, ordering and matching games or for story books featuring the bears from your setting. Preparing for a picnic is a good exercise in organisation and planning.

**Moving on**

## Surprise!

A familiar first toy, the simple pop-up delights babies and holds their attention. The surprise toy develops throughout childhood into 'lift the flap' toys, Jack in the Box, pop up books, treasure chests and other hiding and finding games for older children.

## Young babies (0-11 months)

Soft pop up toys in cones will delight most babies, and some will go on with the game for as long as you care to play! It is easy to make your own from a card cone and a short stick, with a small soft toy fixed to the stick with an elastic band. make the pop up toy appear and disappear from all sorts of places, and practice the 'ready, steady, go' or 'One, two, three' of peek-a-boo games.

### Heads Up, Lookers and Communicators

## Babies (8-20 months)

Babies will still enjoy these simple surprise toys and you can use them as 'bait' to encourage crawling, creeping and walking, to provide a focus and encourage children gently forward. Also use pop-up toys for simple games of peek-a-boo and hide-and-find. Holding a pop-up toy within reach can encourage a sitting baby to practice reaching and grasping as you make the toy appear and disappear. Make sure the toy is securely fixed!

### Sitters, Standers and Explorers

## Young children (16-26 months)

Young children will now be fascinated with the cause and effect of pop-up toys and games. Their hand-eye coordination will be improving, so offer them toys that pop up when you press a button, turn a knob or pull a string. Rows of wooden figures in a frame provide multiple chances to activate the pop, and some make music or talk when activated. Begin to use pop-up puppets for stories, such as a rabbit in a watering can, a bear in a honey pot.

**Movers, Shakers and Players**

## Children (22-36 months)

Some simple hammer toys have a pop-up reaction, as the piece is tapped. This sort of game helps with hand-eye coordination, and some children will play them again and again. Toy pop-up toasters and tills give the same experience. Jack (or Jill)-in-a-box toys are also long term favourites. Children will begin to use pop-up puppets themselves and can make home made pop-ups with soft toys in empty boxes, cartons or tubes.

**Walkers, Talkers and Pretenders**

## Older children (30-60+ months)

At this age, children can, with help, make pop-up puppets and jack-in-the-boxes of their own. This can develop into making and enjoying simple pop-up books, lift-the-flap books and other hidden secrets in craft work and displays. Get some of the little toys with springs and suction caps, which stick to a flat surface and then pop up suddenly, jumping high into the air. Children love the anticipation and the surprise. Make sure children stand clear!

**Moving on**

## Dolls

Dolls are other firm and traditional favourites. Dressing, looking after and taking them along on adventures have engaged children since the time when prehistoric children made dolls from clay or sticks. Stories about dolls are many and varied in all cultures and languages where they often have special powers.

## Young babies (0-11 months)

First dolls are soft, warm and cuddly, they often have simple features and non-removable clothes. First dolls don't need to be very complex, you can make a simple doll by just tying a good, fat knot in the corner of a piece of fleece or towelling, leaving a corner free at the top, and tying smaller knots in two more corners to make hands. The face can either be embroidered or just drawn with permanent marker. These dolls, are safe, cheap and popular.

**Heads Up, Lookers and Communicators**

## Babies (8-20 months)

Dolls for all ages must be washable and should be able to stand up to plenty of hard wear as they are hugged, sucked, carried, dragged and trodden on by babies as they crawl, sit, stand and begin to walk. Simple, soft dolls continue to be popular, but you could add some small baby dolls who can be washed and dried quickly and easily. Begin to use dolls  in simple play such as tea-parties, outings and wrapping activities.

**Sitters, Standers and Explorers**

## Young children (16-26 months)

Tough and hardwearing dolls are still needed at this stage, and you should check regularly to make sure you have dolls from all sorts of cultures and races. Boy and girl dolls should also be added early, when questions about differences can be explored without embarrassment. As children begin to be mobile, offering beds, pushchairs, backpacks, blankets, pillows and other extras will expand the play into caring for and imitating baby care.

### Movers, Shakers and Players

## Children (22-36 months)

All sorts of dolls will be popular with different groups at different times. Some will be brought to story sessions for holding, some will accompany children to the top of the climbing frame. Putting on and taking off clothes of different sorts will help with fine motor development, and hats, gloves, socks and shoes will add to the fun. Make sure your range of dolls includes different styles and types of hair, clothing and accessories.

### Walkers, Talkers and Pretenders

## Older children (30-60+ months)

During Foundation 1 and 2, children will love to be involved in making fantasy and story clothes for the dolls in your setting - help them to make film character clothing, superhero headbands, wedding clothes, hats. You don't need to be able to sew - fabric glue, pins, staples and wool or string will all help with fixing fabric or paper. Don't forget necklaces, bracelets, watches, bags and other accessories, and involve the boys as well as the girls.

### Moving on

## Persona Dolls

Persona dolls are used to encourage empathy and understanding of others. They have a place in every setting, for use by adults and by children themselves, many becoming characters in their own right with their own personality, history, pleasures, sadness and problems.

## Young babies (0-11 months)

Persona dolls come in several sizes and many types. They also have varied features, skin colours and clothing. Some are smaller, and these are more suitable to use with babies. At first you just need to sit with a baby and introduce the doll. To a small baby, the doll may seem like another baby and they may become fascinated with the face, eyes and other features. This will just let them become familiar with the dolls in preparation for later stages.

### Heads Up, Lookers and Communicators

## Babies (8-20 months)

Small persona dolls have been successfully used with babies in nurseries where the dolls become members of the group. They join the babies for all activities, including snacks meals, stories, rests and play. The babies carry or drag the dolls up slides, into the garden, onto cushions for a rest. The practitioners encourage this use, finding that even young babies can look after the dolls, and that empathy with them is built up over time in the nursery class.

### Sitters, Standers and Explorers

## Young children (16-26 months)

This is the best stage for introducing the persona dolls as characters, with names histories, families, troubles and pleasures. They can be used to explore the first problems and troubles children experience - unhappiness, jealousy, anger, pleasure or celebration. Many persona dolls begin to accumulate a whole family history, which children will begin to remember, so you may find it is often easier to write it down than try to remember!

### Movers, Shakers and Players

## Children (22-36 months)

Sit your persona dolls on a shelf where they can see what is going on when they are not in use by you or the children. Continue to encourage children to take the dolls outside, on visits, for stories or to help them when they feel unsettled. The more you use them, the more the children will empathise with their stories when you use them to explore issues that arise from day to day. Make sure you have several dolls to use, so you can explore different issues.

### Walkers, Talkers and Pretenders

## Older children (30-60+ months)

By this stage, children may well use the dolls themselves as a prompt to explore difficult issues with an adult or in small groups. There are several books of ideas for using these dolls, so if you are unsure of how to use them, get hold of a book to help you, or go on a training course. Keep expanding the family of dolls, either by buying specially made ones or using a newly introduced normal doll, and building a character for them with the children.

### Moving on

## Soft toy animals

These toys are everywhere, from motorway services to fast food outlets, and they are loved by children of all ages and by adults. We see them dangling in cars, hung from babies' prams and cots, piled in baskets and adorning shelves and beds in children's bedrooms. They come in every size and type we can imagine.

## Young babies (0-8 months)

Favourite friends for life are often made at this age. A baby has a dangling teddy above his or her chair or cot and this toy becomes a favourite image throughout childhood. Suspend small soft toy animals from secure strings above playmats, changing beds and cots. A circular indoor washing line with plastic pegs can hold soft toys firmly as they sway gently above the baby. Or you could use key rings made from plastic spirals.

### Heads Up, Lookers and Communicators

## Babies (8-20 months)

Offer babies baskets of different sorts and sizes of soft toy animals. They will often have a favourite size or type. Let them have a soft toy at group time or during stories and changing - this will often be enough to keep a wriggly toddler still while they listen or submit to changing. Bring soft toy animals to story times together, and use them as a focus for relevant stories, they  don't have to be identical to the story character to be a focus.

### Sitters, Standers and Explorers

16

## Young children (16-26 months)

Offering simple beds and covers for soft toys gives further practice in caring for and thinking about others, through familiar everyday activities. Let younger children bring favourite soft toys to group times and snack, or on walks and visits. Small pushchairs and prams will give opportunities to include the toys in outdoor activities and role play. Continue to use small soft toys in stories and in simple sorting and counting activities, where children can handle and arrange them independently.

**Movers, Shakers and Players**

## Children (22-36 months)

Add soft toy pets, such as dogs, cats, birds, hamsters, to role play areas, complete with their beds, carrying baskets, cages, feeding bowls, collars and leads etc. Extend the use of these toys in sorting and counting activities. Include them in bags and baskets for outdoor play and picnics. And every so often, have a soft toy wash day where the children can squeeze them in warm bubbly water and hang them outside to dry.

**Walkers, Talkers and Pretenders**

## Older children (30-60+ months)

At this stage, children can be involved in many role play and imaginative activities such as making a pet shop, toy shop or vet's surgery complete with bandages, pet boxes, injections and medications, exploring the worries of visiting hospitals or doctors themselves. Making houses, beds, furniture or even clothes and hats for soft toys will expand children's technology experience, and using toys such as Beat Baby and Lola the Listening Leopard will improve skills through the use of steady beat and activities for listening.

**Moving on**

17

## Finger Puppets

Finger puppets are an essential resource for practitioners. They have hundreds of uses and can be bought in all sorts of shapes and sizes. Some come in sets, with a glove puppet and one or more associated finger puppets. Collect some animals, story characters, fantasy creatures and people of all sorts.

## Young babies (0-11 months)

Finger puppets are ideal for adult child activities in close, comfortable situations. Try putting one on your finger for a baby to watch and follow as you sing or say a rhyme or tell a little story. The puppets are too small for the baby to use themselves, and the parts may not survive grabbing and sucking, so keep this activity for one-to-one times while babies are very small. You could make finger puppets into a mobile to hang above a changing table or playmat.

**Heads Up, Lookers and Communicators**

## Babies (8-20 months)

As they get older, babies can start to use a finger puppet themselves. Just one on a forefinger will help develop the skill of separating this finger, an essential skill for many later activities. Finger puppet can also fit in pockets, toy cars or small trucks for carrying about and giving rides. They are easily grasped and stuffed into containers of all sorts, and can be used in brick or other construction play. Use them yourself for singing and rhymes.

**Sitters, Standers and Explorers**

## Young children (16-26 months)

Progress to a puppet on each forefinger when they are able to manage both hands. Grab a puppet or two when you are singing or playing finger games and number rhymes. Try and get some sets of finger puppets for Five Little Speckled Frogs, Five Little Ducks etc, or make up your own words to well known songs, so you can use the puppets you have. Use finger puppets in one-to-one sessions with children who have language difficulties to encourage talk.

### Movers, Shakers and Players

## Children (22-36 months)

Begin to incorporate finger puppets in little made-up stories, either with an adult or for children to use themselves. Leave a basket of finger puppets near your story area so children can have one to hold as they listen to stories and songs. This often helps concentration and avoids the fiddling and fidgeting individuals may display. Use the puppets and an empty box to explore vocabulary such as 'in', 'on', 'under', 'behind' etc.

### Walkers, Talkers and Pretenders

## Older children (30-60+ months)

Buy or make some people finger puppets and story characters for your collection, as children at this stage may be able to follow and 'act out' a simple story using the range of puppets. Try with very familiar stories such as the Three Bears, Three Pigs, or Billy Goats Gruff. Explore stories from other cultures and countries and act these out with finger puppets. Try to involve everyone in the group, buy having plenty of animals and people for 'crowd scenes' or to wave and sing at appropriate parts of the story.

### Moving on

## Glove Puppets

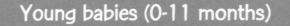

Glove puppets have different uses and need different skills to use them. Some need the hand upright, others need a flat or sideways movement. There are many linked to stories or particular themes, scenes and situations, and some are as big as the children themselves. Glove puppets are just as effective when used without a puppet theatre.

## Young babies (0-11 months)

As with finger puppets, young babies will need you there as they explore these sorts of puppets. You will have to work them, and the baby will be fascinated by the movements, unaware that you are doing it! Some hand puppets have noisy or tactile aspects that babies will enjoy exploring as you hold the puppet securely. Check washability and child friendliness of the types you buy.

**Heads Up, Lookers and Communicators**

## Babies (8-20 months)

Glove puppets will often encourage a timid or quiet child to talk or move. They will still be unaware that you are moving the puppet, and may respond to it, more readily than a person. Pointing, grabbing and gesturing are encouraged by this play. Animal puppets, and those from stories are often favourites, and will be carried or dragged about in the same way as teddies and other soft toys, until the babies realise that they can make them move.

**Sitters, Standers and Explorers**

## Young children (16-26 months)

Glove puppets can now be used in small group activities where the adult uses it to enhance a story or to gain attention. Big puppets, dressed as children, story characters or adults, can also be used to explore familiar situations, worries, concerns and other issues that arise in the setting. These figurative puppets are now an essential part of the equipment and activities of early years settings. If you are anxious about using them, going on a course is very worthwhile.

### Movers, Shakers and Players

## Children (22-36 months)

Add glove puppets to story bags and leave some outside where children can include them in their active play. Adults will find that they can expand the use of bigger hand puppets, such as dogs, cats, bears, monkeys, which are so life-like that they become an additional member of the group. Hand puppets are invaluable for language and counting activities, as they capture attention and can appear to need help from the children.

### Walkers, Talkers and Pretenders

## Older children (30-60+ months)

Older children may now be ready to act out their puppet stories, retelling favourite tales or making up their own. A puppet theatre is not necessary, but a clothes airer or a simple piece of fabric hung across a doorway may encourage more timid children to join in, when they can be unseen players. Hiding a new puppet in your garden with a note for the children gives an opportunity for introducing a new character in your setting.

### Moving on

## Story characters

Puppets, dolls and soft toys have been made to support the telling and increase the enjoyment of many stories and rhymes. Some come in Story Sacks or bags, others are boxed with a book, CD or video. Film characters are marketed for every new children's film or TV programme. They all have their uses and should be welcomed in your setting.

### Young babies (0-11 months)

Using a simple puppet when you tell a story, sing a song, or say a rhyme to a baby is a good way to help focus and enjoyment. Remember that babies focus best at 20-35 cm (8-15 ins), and don't move objects too fast. Help the baby to feel different parts of the toy, stroking, patting, touching with fingers and palms. Use characters to play simple games of 'Round and Round the Garden', 'Peep-bo', 'Two Little Dickey Birds' and other simple songs and rhymes.

### Heads Up, Lookers and Communicators

### Babies (8-20 months)

A 3D version of Kipper, Dogger, Wibbly Pig, Spot, Winnie the Pooh or other story puppet will make a story much more appealing for babies. Keep the story short, and talk about the toy before you begin, so the focus is clear. In one-to-one or very small groups, one child could hold the toys as you read the story. Some children may bring books and toys from home, and these will expand your repertoire of characters to talk about.

### Sitters, Standers and Explorers

## Young children (16-26 months)

Many picture books now have character dolls and figures suitable for this age group. Dinosaur Roar, Farmer Duck and Rainbow Fish are some examples. The character is a good visual key for the children - pass it round before you tell the story, or there may be fidgeting and reaching as the children try to feel the real toy during the story. Character puppets are also useful in retelling stories, and can be used by children later to recreate their own versions.

### Movers, Shakers and Players

## Children (22-36 months)

Brown Bear, Elmer the Elephant, Peter Rabbit and other story book characters will enable you to extend children's experiences by using the theme of the story to link with mathematical, social or other areas of the curriculum, such as exploring colour and shape. Children's TV and films often result in toys with story books - Nemo, Buzz Lightyear, Bob the Builder and Postman Pat are firm favourites, although the stories are often too complex for younger children.

### Walkers, Talkers and Pretenders

## Older children (30-60+ months)

Familiar stories such as the Very Hungry Caterpillar, Bob the Builder or Handa's Surprise can be used with characters and puppets to explore aspects of Knowledge and Understanding of the World such as a sense of time, a sense of place, designing and making or cultures and beliefs. The objects will help to make the theme of the story tangible to the children. Rhymes such as The Old Woman who Swallowed a Fly, and stories such as Snow White can also benefit. Continue to use current favourites from films and TV alongside classic favourites.

### Moving on

## Barbie and friends

Barbie dolls, their friends, families, pets and accessories all give opportunities for play and creativity. They are often reasonably priced, and despite Barbie's stereotypical shape, they have plenty of play value in your setting for boys and girls. Try to get some accessories to extend the play, look in local sales or bargain shops, or on the Internet.

## Young babies (0-11 months)

For babies, Barbie dolls will just be something to look at! The dolls can 'walk' and 'talk' where small babies can see them, but they are not really suitable for handling, due to their sharp edges and removable parts. However, a Barbie-type doll will engage a baby for a while as their eyes play over the different colours and shiny features of the figures.

**Heads Up, Lookers and Communicators**

## Babies (8-20 months)

Babies of this age will play with anything! They are fascinated by anything they can reach, so you will need to control the use of any toys that may present danger due to their small parts and sharp features. Barbie-type dolls have these, so it would be wise to restrict play with these to times when you can supervise carefully. However, exploring Barbie's car or horse  may be an exciting opportunity for a growing baby.

**Sitters, Standers and Explorers**

## Young children (16-26 months)

The desire to be like older children is often a trigger for tantrums at this age. Children love to have toys that are the usual playthings for older brothers and sisters, and this includes Barbie and other teen-type dolls. The accessories and clothes are far too difficult to manage, but Barbie's bathtime or small cardboard boxes for bedtimes will be a good substitute for children who really like playing with such toys. Think carefully before including them - they are part of real life!

### Movers, Shakers and Players

## Children (22-36 months)

This is the stage when imaginative play with dolls begins to be very complex. Children are beginning to explore the world outside their close families, and figures like Barbie are tempting, despite their stereotypical shapes and clothing. Make sure you have a wide range of these dolls, including boy dolls and dolls from different cultures and countries. Add suitable clothing and accessories, and use these to help with fine motor development.

### Walkers, Talkers and Pretenders

## Older children (30-60+ months)

At this point, it is useful to begin the discussion about similarities and differences, and talking about what men and women do. Barbie-type dolls can also be used to inspire house and furniture making. Try to get some doll sets that show Barbie and her friends in stronger, less stereotyped activities - look for Barbie the dentist or doctor, not just Barbie the air steward or nurse. Fantasy play with these dolls is also fun, using recycled materials to make castles, dungeons, mountains, carriages etc.

### Moving on

## Houses and homes

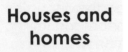 

Doll's houses and other homes have enormous potential for discussion, language learning and play in both adult accompanied and child initiated situations. Exploring similarities and differences, vocabulary and position will make them a favourite toy if sensitively modelled and valued. Don't let your doll's house become a sad and neglected toy.

## Young babies (0-11 months)

A doll's house is a fascinating thing - even little babies will love to look at the tiny objects and dolls. Don't forget that their focus is at about 25cm (12ins), so hold them close, or hold the objects close to them. Holding a tiny doll will be a reflex, but useful all the same.

**Heads Up, Lookers and Communicators**

## Babies (8-20 months)

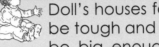

Doll's houses for this age need to be tough and the pieces need to be big enough to be held and played with, without being damaged or swallowed. Simple houses without fronts or backs are best, and chunky wooden furniture will resist knocks. Don't put too many things in the house, just a few objects and people, and leave it on the floor for a crawling baby or on a low table for those who are beginning to stand. Sit with them as they play and talk.

**Sitters, Standers and Explorers**

## Young children (16-26 months)

Fascination with miniatures often emerges at this age, and children will play with small versions of household furniture and dolls, specially if you are there to talk and play alongside. Don't have too much furniture and make sure dolls houses are easy to get into - frustration will emerge if chidlren's hands get in the way and knock over their own little arrangements. Remember to have dolls of all ages, races and cultures right from the start.

### Movers, Shakers and Players

## Children (22-36 months)

Ready made castles, forts, towers, caves, zoos and other fantasy places are all different sorts of 'dolls houses'. Encourage all sorts of play with these, using small world figures of knights, spacemen, fantasy figures and animals. You will probably find some children will just use them for the domestic play they have experience of, and this may well be by making the fantasy place into a home, complete with tea!

### Walkers, Talkers and Pretenders

## Older children (30-60+ months)

Fantasy play, making homes and environments from boxes and cartons for figures and animals is a great way to expand manual skills and creativity. Castles, caves, pirate ships, blocks of flats, even Tracey Island will be a great project for children with adult help. Make plenty of doors and windows, and remember that children are not worried about exact scale at this stage! Some children will be able to manage smaller objects and figures, and may become fascinated by tiny houses and homes, for Play People, Polly Pocket or Sylvanian Families.

### Moving on

## Sound and music

Many modern toys talk, make sounds, move in response to touch or talk, or play music. They have many uses in spontaneous play and more structured activities. From baby gym toys to computer links, they are attention grabbers and will delight most babies and children, who will persevere with actions, however challenging, to get the toys to respond.

## Young babies (0-11 months)

Baby gyms and toys often have music or other sounds incorporated within them. Some make sounds when touched or moved, others need to be wound up by an adult, and some respond to movement. These are often the first toys that babies can work for themselves, but they mostly learn through chance! Watching and helping is important, making sure the baby can reach, but not get tangled in the strings.

### Heads Up, Lookers and Communicators

## Babies (8-20 months)

Bells in balls, 'clatterpillars', trains that chug and toot, and mats and boxes that respond to their movement and touch will fascinate babies as they begin to move under their own steam. Toys that work by pulling strings, pressing buttons and squeezing are popular, but babies are still entranced by the toys and music boxes that are activated by adults. Try  these near changing tables or snack areas as well as places where babies rest and relax.

### Sitters, Standers and Explorers

## Young children (16-26 months)

Pushing, rolling, stamping, hammering are all movements being perfected now. Mats that play music when you stamp, soft toys that talk when you squeeze them or clap at them, books that make noises when you press buttons, will all attract young children. Some soft toys claim to teach children to count and recognise sounds, but most experts would say that a simple children's tape recorder or CD player is a better way to learn.

### Movers, Shakers and Players

## Children (22-36 months)

Try hanging bells and other noise makers such as old cutlery or pots and pans from fences and bushes outside. Indoors, you may like to get some of the soft toy characters that incorporate story tapes and give the children something to cuddle as they listen to favourite stories. Simple response toys such as those from Leapfrog are often introduced at this stage, but should never be used by children without adult support.

### Walkers, Talkers and Pretenders

## Older children (30-60+ months)

Many toys for older children combine the appeal of a soft toy and the claim to be a 'learning toy'. Evaluate these carefully - some may be too advanced for the stated age and may encourage children to be static when they should be active. Choose musical toys that encourage movement and interaction. Touch screen soft toys (looking like a Teletubby with a screen in their tummy) have more flexibility, and give some control to the child. Continue to use all forms of soft toys that respond to movement or action, and discuss how they work.

### Moving on

## Superheroes

Superman, Spiderman, Buzz and friends are favourite toys for most young boys. Some superheroes promote violent and angry responses, but if you choose carefully, many are forces for good and can be used to help children to explore their feelings of frustration and anger though doll play instead of physical violence.

## Young babies (0-11 months)

Even very young babies will respond to the bright colours of these toys, and will follow them as they move. There are soft versions of many of the superheroes from popular children's TV series and films, and these are sometimes preferred to the more traditional toys such as teddies and dolls. Do your homework, and right from the beginning, encourage superheroes (both male and female) that promote good rather than violence.

**Heads Up, Lookers and Communicators**

## Babies (8-20 months)

As babies begin to move under their own steam, they become able to choose their own toys, and the bright colours of these figures will still attract attention. The admiration for older siblings and children in your setting may also begin to influence choice of toys. At this age the fascination factor will be the toy itself, not the role the character plays on the screen or in comics. Just grasping a superhero and carrying it with them may be enough.

**Sitters, Standers and Explorers**

## Young children (16-26 months)

Superheroes begin to fly, talk and ride with young children as they get on the move. Many children, specially some boys will spend hours flying a superhero around in their hand, role playing through the little figure. As long as this play is sensitively managed, superhero play is good for letting off steam and developing the imagination. Start to talk about superhero play at this stage, so children know you value it and will recognise it.

**Movers, Shakers and Players**

## Children (22-36 months)

At this stage, full body superhero play may well increase. Channel this by restricting the area for play or by substituting toys for the whole body play. Superhero areas outside and indoors can be made exciting with drapes, big bricks, boxes and other structures. Remember to include female superheroes as well, and make a clear boundary between those who do good and the ones that encourage simple violence. You may need to restrict the play to using toys belonging to the setting.

**Walkers, Talkers and Pretenders**

## Older children (30-60+ months)

During this stage, children are subject to a testosterone surge that has a more visible effect in many boys. The result is superhero play of all sorts, specially in those boys most affected, involving them in games of danger, rescue, strength and heroics, and ignoring or banning such play will not make it go away! Providing suitable toys and accessories will help, as long as you are clear about boundaries and talk about the play. Try superhero headbands of all colours to wear while playing with superhero toys, and challenges for making vehicles, clothes, buildings.

**Moving on**

## Bathtime

Bathtime, dressing and undressing dolls and other toys involves many skills and is a key to developing fine motor skills in young children. If you vary the situation, the type of doll and the activity, children will maintain their interest and return to these activities again and again with pleasure as they grow older.

### Young babies (0-11 months)

Bathtime toys and dolls are very popular with babies. Don't worry about dressing and undressing, just sitting in a bowl or bath of warm bubbly water with a washable doll will expand the baby's experiences and enjoyment. Never leave a baby or small child in a bath alone.

**Heads Up, Lookers and Communicators**

### Babies (8-20 months)

Offer this play in a shallow tray or paddling pool. Add a few babies in just their nappies, and a doll each for washing, splashing and dunking! A few bubbles or a bit of shampoo can be added, so hair can be washed. Flannels are essential and very good for developing finger and grasping control as the babies wash their babies. Supervise this play at all times, wet babies and wet surfaces are very slippery, specially if you use bubbles.

**Sitters, Standers and Explorers**

## Young children (16-26 months)

Fill your water tray with warm, bubbly water (put it outside or on a big bath towel to absorb the inevitable spills). Add some dolls, flannels, towels, talc and clothes and stand back while the play begins. Young children love water play of all sorts, and baby bathtime will become a favourite. Younger children may need help with drying and dressing the dolls after their baths and others will not want to stop washing, so be sensitive to their needs and different styles of learning.

### Movers, Shakers and Players

## Children (22-36 months)

Continue to offer regular bathtime play at this stage, gradually making it more complex. Children can add their own bubbles, do their own undressing of the dolls, make decisions about the sorts of clothes to dress them in after their baths. Make sure the fastenings on clothes are easy to do, and there are plenty to choose from. Offer beds, pushchairs and prams for the clean babies, and add blankets, pillows and sheets.

### Walkers, Talkers and Pretenders

## Older children (30-60+ months)

At this stage, baby or doll bathing should give lots of opportunities for talking and developing concepts of sequence and order of dressing, undressing, washing hair, drying and dressing. Children could be asked to tell you the order they need to do things in before they start, and recall them after the event. Washing activities can expand to clothes washing and drying, and the sequences these involve. Hang a washing line outside on a windy day and talk about how the wind dries the clothes. Tell washing line stories such as The Wind Blew, and Mrs Mopple.

### Moving on

## Teaparties

Social play with cups of tea and food will engage most children, whatever their background or culture. Providing plenty of free access to these materials, and joining in to model behaviour is a key way that practitioners can help children develop social skills, turn taking and conversation.

## Young babies (0-11 months)

The beginnings of teaparties are based on little exchanges between babies and adults as they pass things to each other. As you prepare food for babies, make sure they can see what you are doing, and as you feed them, talk about what is happening. Use the politenesses of please and thank you, even though they don't understand the words, they will get used to the tone you use. Let them play with plastic cups, beakers and plates, so they get used to handling them.

**Heads Up, Lookers and Communicators**

## Babies (8-20 months)

As soon as babies can grasp and let go, offer them simple plastic cups, spoons and plates from doll's teasets, so they can feed teddies and other toys. Letting go needs much more control and practice, so the teasets are better empty! Offering cups of tea or pretend food to toys and humans is one of the first social activities that babies get involved in and sometimes they get obsessed with it. Providing a teddy, larger sized soft toy or a big puppet is often a help.

**Sitters, Standers and Explorers**

## Young children (16-26 months)

Offering teasets (cups, jugs, plates and teapots) in your water tray will give plenty of practice in pouring, filling and emptying. Discourage drinking though! Young children will still bring you cups of tea throughout their time in your setting, and you need to be constantly ready to receive them gracefully, even when you are evidently busy with something else. Adult initiated teaparties with soft toys and dolls are very useful for first counting, matching and one-to-one work.

**Movers, Shakers and Players**

## Children (22-36 months)

The simple plastic teasets used in domestic play are familiar in most settings, try alternatives, such as Asian metal food containers, plastic boxes, real cups and mugs, picnic baskets or small rucksacks for outdoor play, or a group picnic with all the children, their toys and dolls. These events can be pretend parties, but they are much more fun with real snacks and fruit, and real juice instead of tea. These can be part of skills development.

**Walkers, Talkers and Pretenders**

## Older children (30-60+ months)

As children get older, you will need to expand the play resources in role play areas, so children continue to develop their play. Otherwise play can descend into aimless routines and repetition of previous stages. Spice up the play by making sure there are plenty of food related objects - saucepans, wooden spoons, baby bottles, trainer cups, mugs, bowls and implements for feeding babies, as well as pet bowls and pet food. Chopping real vegetables, cooking, or making snacks together in the home corner can also rejuvenate interest for the children.

**Moving on**

## DIY dolls

You don't need to buy expensive dolls for children to have fun and enter the world of doll play. Simple materials and a bit of imagination is all you need to support the making and enjoying of a wide variety of home made dolls. And as children get beyond babyhood, they can make their own dolls from familiar objects, using their emerging skills.

## Young babies (0-11 months)

The best home - made dolls for babies are soft, cuddly and not too big. They can be made without sewing by simply tying a big knot in a piece of soft fabric, or putting a soft ball or piece of foam in the middle of the fabric and tying it securely with a soft cord. You can then make 'hands' and 'feet' by knotting the corners, and a face by drawing features in permanent marker or by embroidery. These dolls don't need hair or clothes.

**Heads Up, Lookers and Communicators**

## Babies (8-20 months)

Simple cloth dolls continue to be popular with babies, and you can vary the type by making long eared rabbits, round eared teddies by tying or binding different parts of thin fleece or washable fabric. Using animal patterned fleece (spots, stripes or colours) can widen your imaginative range, and using strong elastic bands will make the job easier. Add some bells or jingles inside the ears or feet to make a little sound when the doll or toy is shaken.

**Sitters, Standers and Explorers**

## Young children (16-26 months)

Simple, small dolls of all shapes, colours and sizes made from tights, socks or other pieces of fabric stuffed with washable foam or man made wadding will engage young children in small world play. They can be carried easily, don't damage when dropped, sucked or left out in the rain. They can ride in toy cars, pushchairs and other vehicles, sit on branches, slide down slides and even act as first 'throw and catch' games, as it is easier to grab their arms and legs than a ball or other smooth object.

**Movers, Shakers and Players**

## Children (22-36 months)

Doll making with recycled materials can start at this age, when children can dress a simple framework of sticks (lolly sticks or garden sticks) using scraps of felt or fabric, wool for hair, and decorations such as buttons or beads. These dolls will be well loved and will encourage creativity and role play if they have home made beds, covers and other furniture. Rice or small dried beans can also turn socks into dolls just by tying, filling and decorating.

**Walkers, Talkers and Pretenders**

## Older children (30-60+ months)

At this stage, many children have sufficient control to make dolls from pipe cleaners with a bit of help. You can thread a bead on the first pipe cleaner to make a head, then add arms and legs, and stick on clothes and hair. Children may then like to make a house for their dolls to live in. Use some cartons or other boxes to make the house, and furnish it with doll's house furniture. Or you could make a fantasy home such as a castle or cave. You can also use simple ready made objects such as bean bags to make toys - just offer wool, felt, little stickers, buttons for features, legs, hair etc.

**Moving on**

## Make your own puppets

Making puppets is another way to help develop manual dexterity in a creative way. Model making and playing with simple puppets where children can see you and get used to the enjoyment of this simple activity. Then they will begin to spontaneously make their own simple puppets in free play and incorporate them in games and stories.

## Young babies (0-11 months)

The best first puppets for babies are very simple. Draw a simple black line face on a paper plate, and fix this firmly to a short stick. Even very tiny babies will respond to these face puppets if you hold them where they can focus, and move them slowly so the baby can follow. Other simple home made puppets can be made from cones of felt or thin card with faces and ears, slotted on the end of your fingers and gently moved in the baby's field of vision.

**Heads Up, Lookers and Communicators**

## Babies (8-20 months)a

The important concept of moving individual fingers to make puppets move should be encouraged as soon as babies can wave and point. Sticking little stickers and stars to individual fingers, or even every finger makes this first movement fun. Also try drawing faces on hands and toes with felt pen or face paint, so fingers and toes become little puppets.  Make faces on your own fingers too, so they can talk together or sing songs and rhymes.

**Sitters, Standers and Explorers**

## Young children (16-26 months)

Home made puppets for young children can be made very simply from everyday materials. Draw or paint faces on upside down paper bags, then stuff them with scrunched up paper and tie a string or thin elastic round the open end to make a first string puppet. Push pencils or short sticks into cheap foam balls and add faces and hair. Children don't need a puppet theatre to have fun with puppets, just some friends and space to play.

### Movers, Shakers and Players

## Children (22-36 months)`

Make cone and tube finger puppets from card, several for each child, and leave them to decorate them however they wish to make people, fantasy characters, animals or birds. Try turning old socks into puppets by attaching eyes and other features such as hair, feathers, big ears etc. It's best to practice using the sock first, then mark where the eyes and mouth need to be with felt pen so the children know where they go.

### Walkers, Talkers and Pretenders

## Older children (30-60+ months)

As the children get more practiced at designing and making, they can use many objects for puppets - cheap wooden spoons, paper plates on sticks, paper bags, plastic cups, and gloves or mittens (perhaps from your Lost Property Box!). Cut the fingers off gloves, seal the ends with glue and make each finger into a different puppet. Take digital photos of the children and print them out so they can make a puppet of their own face by mounting the picture on a card circle on a lollipop stick. These puppets are great fun as children pretend to be each other or themselves.

### Moving on

# Existing and planned titles in the Baby and Beyond series include:

* Messy Play (ready now)
* Sensory Experiences (ready now)
* Music and Sound (ready now)
* The Natural World (ready now)
* Construction (ready now)
* Marks & Mark Making (ready now)
* Dolls and Soft Toys (ready now)
* Bikes, Prams & Pushchairs (ready)
* Finger Songs and Rhymes (ready)

* Role Play (ready now)
* Food and Cooking (2008)
* Dens, Shelters and Play outside (2008)
* Counting (2008)
* Small World Play (2008)
* Tell me a Story (2008)
* Riding Together (2008)
* Movement and Beat (2008)
* Going Out (2008)